CHI

ACPL ITEM

DISCARDED

S0-ATG-087

DO NOT REMOVE
CARDS FROM POCKET

JAN 1 4 1997

ALLEN COUNTY PUBLIC LIBRARY
FORT WAYNE, INDIANA 46802

You may return this book to any agency, branch,
or bookmobile of the Allen County Public Library.

DEMCO

# Read All About Numbers

# NUMBERS AND
# AGE

## John M. Patten, Jr., Ed.D.

The Rourke Corporation, Inc.
Vero Beach, Florida 32964

© 1996 The Rourke Corporation, Inc.

Allen County Public Library
900 Webster Street
PO Box 2270
Fort Wayne, IN 46801-2270

All rights reserved. No part of this book may be reproduced or utilized in any form or by any means, electronic or mechanical including photocopying, recording or by any information storage and retrieval system without permission in writing from the publisher.

John M. Patten, Jr. Ed.D.
25 years of professional experience as a writer, elementary and secondary school teacher, elementary school principal and K-12 system wide director of curriculum.
    B.A.—English and social studies; M.ED.—Guidance and education; ED.D.—Education

MATH CONSULTANT:
Mrs. Barbara Westfield, M.S. — Grade Three Teacher

PHOTO CREDITS
Cover, page 10 © John Patten; pages 4, 6, 7, 9, 12, 13, 18, 19, 22 courtesy of Corel; page 16 © C. McClare, U. S. Fish and Wildlife Service; pages 15, 21 © Zack Thomas

**Library of Congress Cataloging-in-Publication Data**

Patten, J. M., 1944-
    Numbers and age / by John M. Patten, Jr.
        p.  cm. — (Read all about numbers)
    Includes index.
    Summary: Explains that age is indicated in terms of numbers and determined by counting: then shows that age is measured in time periods, generations, and life spans.
        ISBN 0-86593-437-1
    1. Aging—Juvenile literature.   2. Age—Juvenile literature. [1. Aging.
2. Age.]
I. Title  II. Series: Patten, J. M., 1944-   Read all about numbers
QP86.P35 1996
612.6—dc20                                             96–12629
                                                                 CIP
                                                                 AC

**Printed in the USA**

# TABLE OF CONTENTS

## AGE IS NUMBERS

How old are you? When is your birthday? When were you born?

People hear these questions a lot. Also, they are questions you ask your friends.

We often wonder how old somebody or something is. Let's read about **age** (AIJ) and find out how old some things are.

*And how old are you now?*

# FIND AGE BY COUNTING

Age is the amount of time that has passed since birth or the beginning. It is usually counted in years.

This makes grandmothers and grandfathers older than moms and dads. Children are younger because fewer years have gone by since they were born.

*Parents, of course, are older than their children.*

*To run for President, a U.S. citizen must be at least 35 years old.*

If you are now seven years old, you will be eight on your next birthday. Ten years from that birthday you will be age 18.

As people **mature** (meh TYOOR), or grow older, they can do more and more things. A five year old can start school. At 18, you are old enough to vote in elections, get a job or go to college. At 35, a man or woman can be president of the United States.

# HOW DOES AGE ADD UP?

Age is told in **time periods** (TIME PEER ee edz) like days, weeks, months, and years. Three-day-old bread, a three-week-old puppy, a three-month-old baby, and a thirty-year-old teacher—these are all ways of telling age.

A day is 24 hours, weeks are seven days long and a year is about 365 days, or 52 weeks, long.

Many of the 12 months that make up a calendar year have different numbers of days. Many people use this old poem to remember:

Thirty days has September;
April, June and November;
All the rest have thirty-one,
except February alone,
which has but twenty-eight, in fine,
till leap years gives it twenty-nine.

*The months of spring bring beautiful flowers.*

3 1833 02965 9973

## DECADE, CENTURY, MILLENNIUM

A **decade** (DEK aid) is a period of ten years. Four decades is 10+10+10+10 (10 x 4) or 40 years. How many decades long is 80 years?

A **century** (SEN che ree) is 100 years. Four centuries is 100+100+100+100 (100 x 4) or 400 years. How many centuries is a thousand years?

A **millennium** (meh LEN ee um) is one thousand years.

*Water has flowed over these rocks for thousands of years.*

## AGE AND LIFE STAGES

**Life stages** (LIFE STAY jez) are periods of time or different ages in a life. They are based on how old you are.

Infancy is the earliest life stage—the baby times. Childhood is the next life stage, beginning with walking and talking, and lasting until the teenage years. The teen stage is from age 13 to 19.

*This child is in the infant life stage.*

*An old man with some pigeons.*

Teenagers grow to adulthood. Adulthood is usually divided into at least two more life stages.

The life stage between 45 and 60 is called middle age. Sometime after middle age comes old age.

# GENERATIONS AND AGE

Another way to think of age is by generations. A **generation** (jen eh RAY shen) is made up of people born in the same time period.

Grandparents and people around their age belong to one generation. Your parents and their friends make up another generation. You and your friends are in your own generation.

About 25 to 30 years usually separates one generation from another. A family with great-grandparents, grandparents, parents and children has four generations.

*These children are in the same generation.*

Thirty days has Septem
April, June and Novemb
the rest have thir
hich has but
in fine.
leap Year gives it

## AGE AND LIFE SPANS

A **life span** (LIFE span) is all the time between birth and death. This time is different for all living things.

Today, the normal life span for a healthy person in the U.S. is 75 years and more, with many, many people living longer. The expected life span of a cat is 12 to 17 years and a dog from 8 to 14 years, depending on the breed, or kind. Some tortoises live for over 100 years.

Most insects live a few weeks, while some live less than 24 hours. The oldest known living thing is the bristlecone pine tree. Some are over 4,500 years old.

*Some tortoises live for 100 years.*

# HOW OLD IS REALLY OLD?

Age can be counted in thousands, millions, and even billions of years.

Our sun and the planets of our solar system are **ancient** (AIN shent), or of very great age. **Geologists** (jee AHL eh jists), scientists who study the earth, think the earth may be over three billion years old.

*The earth and the moon are very old.*

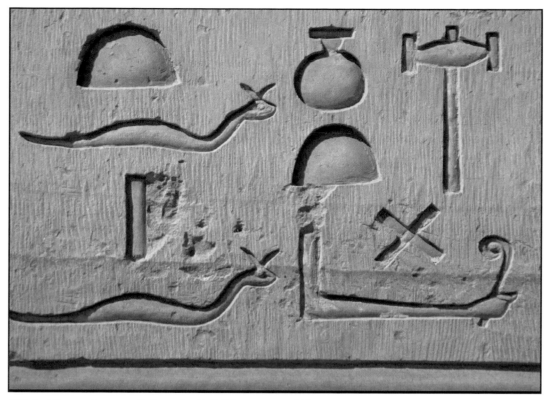

*This Egyptian writing is 5,000 years old.*

The great dinosaurs lived from 245 million years ago until 65 million years ago. This time is called "the age of dinosaurs."

Humans first learned to use fire about 750,000 years ago and to write about 5,000 years ago. In 1996 the United States of America was 220 years old.

## WHAT AGE CAN TELL YOU

People often ask how old someone or something is. Lots of information is found in the answer to the question "How old is it?"

Example: Mom just said someone is coming to spend the afternoon with you. You ask, "How old is this person?" Mom says, "Almost two years old." What does this tell you about your guest?

Example: You need a bicycle. Your friend finds one for sale. You learn that it is 42 years old. What does that tell you about the bike?

Age tells us useful information. What examples can you think of?

*Antique shops sell old things, not new bicycles.*

# 2872 FREDERICK'S ANTIQUES

## WE BUY DAILY!

* QUILTS    * ANTIQUE FURNITURE
* ORIENTAL RUGS    * PAINTINGS

# GLOSSARY

**age** (AIJ) — amount of time that has passed from birth, or the beginning

**ancient** (AIN shent) — of very great age

**century** (SEN che ree) — period of 100 years

**decade** (DEK aid) — period of ten years

**geologists** (jee AHL eh jists) — scientists who study the Earth

**generation** (jen eh RAY shen) — group of people born about the same time

**life span** (LIFE span) — all the time between birth and death

**life stages** (LIFE STAY jez) — periods of time or different ages in life

**mature** (meh TYOOR) — grow older

**millennium** (meh LEN ee um) — period of 1,000 years

**time periods** (TIME PEER ee edz) — days, weeks, months, years

*This desert land formation is thousands of years old.*

# INDEX